In Great
NUMBERS

How Numbers Shape the
World We Live In

Illustrated by Daniela Olejníková

Written by Isabel Thomas, Robert Klanten,
Maria-Elisabeth Niebius, and Raphael Honigstein

LITTLE
GESTALTEN

Navigation

2000 BC

1000 BC

Sumer 4500 BC to 1900 BC

Babylonia 1895 BC to 539 BC

Ancient Greece 800 BC to 146 BC

Ancient Rome 753 BC to 476 AD

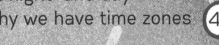

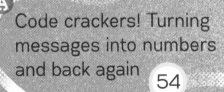
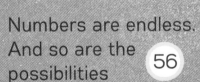

Birth of Jesus

1000 AD

French Revolution 1789

World War II 1939 to 1945

2000 AD

A world without numbers is unthinkable

Numbers are everywhere. They help us make sense of the world—and using them makes our lives easier.

Almost everything can be better understood by looking closely at the numbers hiding beneath the surface. The study of numbers is called mathematics. By revealing the patterns and relationships between numbers, mathematics has enabled us to discover the history of the universe and everything in it, from the birth of giant planets to the behavior of tiny ants.

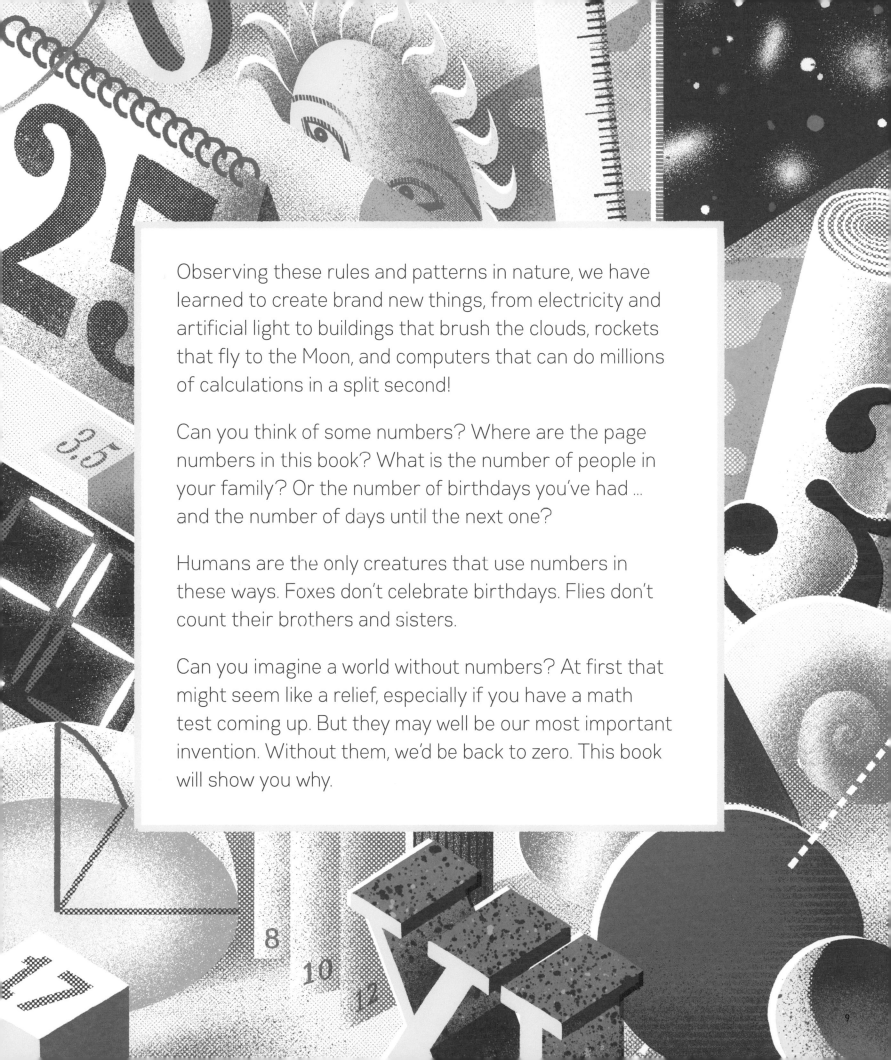

Observing these rules and patterns in nature, we have learned to create brand new things, from electricity and artificial light to buildings that brush the clouds, rockets that fly to the Moon, and computers that can do millions of calculations in a split second!

Can you think of some numbers? Where are the page numbers in this book? What is the number of people in your family? Or the number of birthdays you've had ... and the number of days until the next one?

Humans are the only creatures that use numbers in these ways. Foxes don't celebrate birthdays. Flies don't count their brothers and sisters.

Can you imagine a world without numbers? At first that might seem like a relief, especially if you have a math test coming up. But they may well be our most important invention. Without them, we'd be back to zero. This book will show you why.

The universal language of numbers

All over the world, people use numbers according to the same basic rules for addition, subtraction, multiplication, and division.

2 + 2 is always 4. 5 - 3 is always 2. 3 × 3 is always 9. 10 ÷ 2 is always 5. Because everybody understands and accepts these rules, numbers are like a language that is spoken across the globe.

You can play simple games with numbers that create all kinds of surprises. Try this one — it was spotted by an Indian mathematician called D. R. Kaprekar. It always works, whichever way you try it!

Step 1

Choose a four-digit number (use at least two different digits).

Step 2

Arrange the digits in order of largest to smallest, then smallest to largest.

9743   3479

Step 3

Subtract the smaller number from the larger one.

$9743 - 3479 = 6264$

Step 4

Repeat steps 2 and 3 — this may take up to seven rounds.

$6642 - 2466 = 4176$
$7641 - 1467 = 6174$

No matter what number you start with, you'll always end up with 6,174 — known as Kaprekar's constant. **Give it a go!**

6174

Why even animals can count

You learned to count with your fingers when you were young and can easily do sums by now. You can probably also figure out which is the the larger of two piles of sweets in an instant! This ability to compare quantities with one quick look is called number sense. We have it as newborns, and it gets better as we grow up.

Many animals have strong number sense, too. It's useful in different ways.

Coots keep track of the number of eggs they have laid. If another egg suddenly appears–laid by a lazy bird that wants someone else to feed its chick–they reject it.

Orb-weaving spiders seem to count the prey caught in their webs. In one experiment, scientists removed flies they had caught while the spiders weren't looking. The more flies they removed, the longer the spiders searched for them!

Just one glance is enough for a female mosquito fish to tell the difference between groups of three or four fish. They join the bigger group, which means they will be less likely to be eaten by passing predators!

Before attacking a rival group, spotted hyenas stand back and listen out for the number of different calls. Not the bravest of animals, they only approach groups that are smaller than theirs so that they are sure of winning the fight!

Two goats for one sack of grain? Why numbers became necessary for trade

Imagine you have a handful of sweets and your friend has some chocolate bars that you really, really like. If he's in the same room as you, swapping a few of your sweets for some of his chocolate is quickly done. You can both see exactly what the other one has, and can work out a fair deal that leaves both of you happy.

But if you wanted to do the same trade with a friend over the phone, it would be much more complicated. For that, you need to have language to describe the quantity of sweets to make a fair trade. Trading goods with people from faraway places was the challenge that brought about the use of numbers and measurements.

From small ...

When everyone was living in villages, it was easy to communicate. At first, counting was used for simple activities, such as adding up the number of fish caught at sea, the number of animals in a herd, or the number of steps from one end of a field to the other.

... to big

As towns and cities grew in size, people needed quicker and easier ways to keep track of even larger numbers. When people started traveling from one village to another, and began sharing or selling their crops, the development of numbers and measurements became a necessity.

The earliest-recorded systems of weights and measures originated 5,000 to 6,000 years ago. At first, people living in a village didn't travel far. Each community and region had their own ways of measuring length, volumes, and masses. Beyond that, volume measures for grains were completely separate from those for liquids, cloth was measured very differently from farmland. People wanting to trade their crops or crafts with others farther away needed to find a language of numbers that everyone understood. The solution to this problem was to find standards for weights and measures. Once everyone agreed on the same unit, adding a number made it possible to buy and sell goods with confidence.

So where did our ideas about numbers come from? What was the world like before 1, 2, 3 . . . ? Let's go back a few thousand years and see how ancient peoples started to use numbers.

Hands, sticks, and boards:
how did ancient peoples count?

Over the past few thousand years, different civilizations around the globe developed unique ways of using numbers, which ultimately inspired the one we use today.

As people counted, they kept track using their fingers and toes, or by making marks on suitable objects: ancient animal bones have been found marked with notches, like a rather grim tally chart. The problem with keeping a tally (making one mark for each object counted) is that you can run out of space quite quickly.

The Sumerians
About 6,000 years ago

The Sumerian people were great inventors. They came up with the wheel, farming, and even writing. As their region, Mesopotamia (modern-day Iraq), grew larger and more powerful, Sumerian culture spread far and wide, and they needed to keep a record of very large numbers. They used a system that was based on the number 60. Today, our mathematical order is based on 10, but the Sumerian 60 didn't vanish completely—see if you can find it later in the book.

The Babylonians
About 4,000 years ago

All of Mesopotamia had been conquered by a different people: the Babylonians. Babylon became the capital city of southern Mesopotamia for more than 1,000 years. The Babylonians used the same written language invented by the Sumerians, called cuneiform, and also counted using base 60.

The ancient Romans

About 2,500 years ago

One of the most famous number systems is the one that was used in ancient Rome. The Roman numerals were images of what your hands look like when you count to 10. But this system did not work well for bigger numbers that needed more than two hands.

The Romans therefore used counting boards, or abacuses, to help with their sums. Little stones or "counters" were moved around a board until their final position showed the right answer.

The ancient Chinese

About 3,500 years ago

Some of the earliest civilizations counted using small objects such as sticks. They could move them from one pile to another to make these tally marks either smaller or bigger. Instead of having one stick per object, the ancient Chinese began to display numbers larger than 5 by changing the position of the sticks.

From 0 to 9: the set of 10 symbols we use as numbers today

While the Romans stuck to their counting boards, people elsewhere in the world continued to develop number systems that helped them count, weigh, and measure things quickly and accurately. About 1,500 years ago in India, mathematicians created a set of 10 symbols, to represent the numbers 0 to 9. The big invention by the Indians was the 0, which gave void a number– imagine no sweets in a bowl. This number system is called the decimal system and quickly became very popular.

These symbols weren't based on tally marks or sticks, they were just images, in the same way that an "a" is an abstract symbol that represents the sound "ah."

This is how the pictures created by Hindus look from 0 to 9:

Gradually, these symbols spread to the Middle East and beyond, and were transformed into this:

Each culture that used them adapted the way the numerals were written:

Eventually they became the numerals we use today. They are known as Hindu-Arabic numerals:

Hindu *1,500 years ago until today*	०	१	२	३	४	५	६	७	८	९
Arabic *1,200 years ago until today*	٠	١	٢	٣	٤	٥	٦	٧	٨	٩
Medieval Europe *900 years ago*	0	ı	2	3	௨	௯	6	௮	8	9
Western World *today*	0	1	2	3	4	5	6	7	8	9

Try looking at the columns from top to bottom. Can you see the gradual evolution of each numeral?

Hindu-Arabic numerals are now used almost all over the world. Here is why: these 10 digits can be used to write any number you can think of, no matter how big it is.

Two digits can show the number of children in your class.

Three digits can show the number of pupils in your school.

Five digits can show the number of people in a football stadium.

Seven digits can show the number of people in a city.

If you tried to write the world's population using tally marks, the line would stretch 76 km (47 mi)! Not very practical.

And 10 digits can show the number of people in the world.

Good with numbers:
meet the clever people who invented mathematics

Believe it or not, the rules for the use of numbers you learn in your math classes today were set up hundreds of years ago by very smart people. They loved studying number patterns and liked nothing better than an impossible problem.

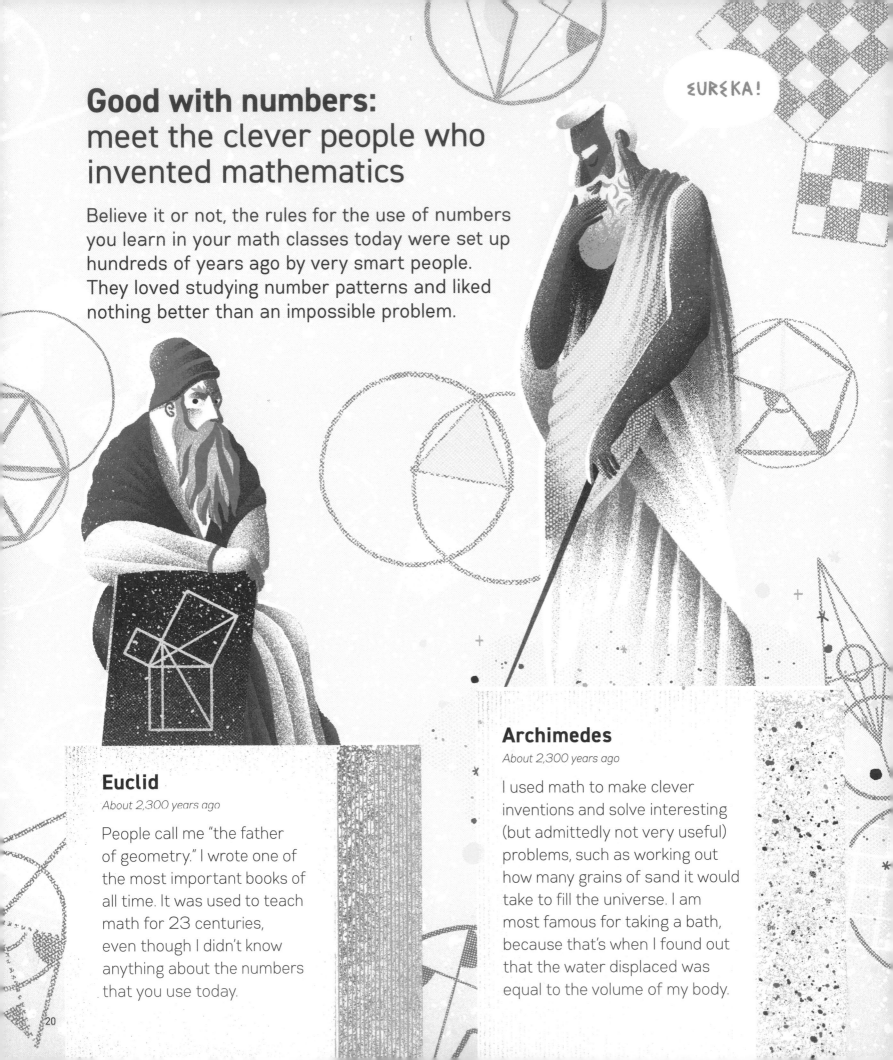

EUREKA!

Euclid
About 2,300 years ago

People call me "the father of geometry." I wrote one of the most important books of all time. It was used to teach math for 23 centuries, even though I didn't know anything about the numbers that you use today.

Archimedes
About 2,300 years ago

I used math to make clever inventions and solve interesting (but admittedly not very useful) problems, such as working out how many grains of sand it would take to fill the universe. I am most famous for taking a bath, because that's when I found out that the water displaced was equal to the volume of my body.

Hypatia of Alexandria

About 1,650 years ago

I was the first notable female mathematician in history and the greatest of my time. Students traveled from far and wide to hear me talk about math, astronomy, and philosophy.

Brahmagupta

About 1,400 years ago

I developed rules for using 0 just like any other number in sums. For example, what happens if you subtract 0 from a positive number (3-0=3) or from a negative number (-3-0=-3). This made lots of new calculations possible.

21

Arms, hands, and seeds: how the first measurements were based on nature

With the growth of civilizations came the need for measurements to help with the trade of goods such as fruits, vegetables, animals, and honey. The first measurements were derived from people's bodies and the world around them.

The **cubit** was the unit of measurement used by the ancient Egyptians. It was based on the length of a person's forearm from the elbow to the tip of the middle finger.

The **pace** was a Roman unit of length, the distance of a stride from where one heel left the ground to where it touched down again. A Roman **mile** was 1,000 paces.

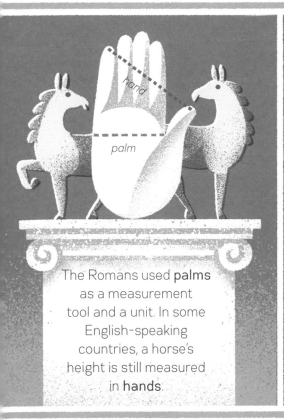

The Romans used **palms** as a measurement tool and a unit. In some English-speaking countries, a horse's height is still measured in **hands**.

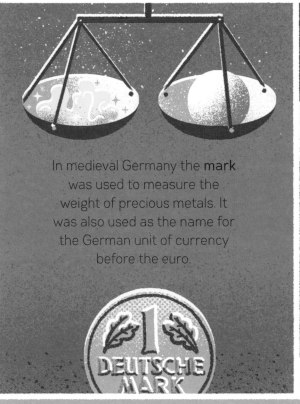

In medieval Germany the **mark** was used to measure the weight of precious metals. It was also used as the name for the German unit of currency before the euro.

1
DEUTSCHE
MARK

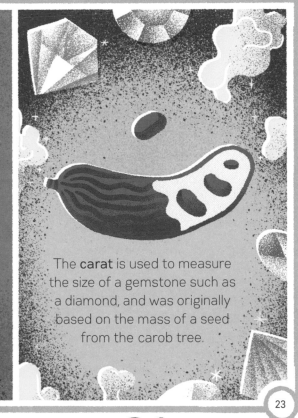

The **carat** is used to measure the size of a gemstone such as a diamond, and was originally based on the mass of a seed from the carob tree.

A new, easier system:
modern ways of measuring

For hundreds of years, different units of measurement were used to buy and sell goods. This could be chaotic, confusing, and open to cheating. To make things more fair and, as we learned, to help civilizations grow, rulers gradually began to introduce standard systems of weights and measurements.

A revolutionary system

After the French Revolution in 1789, the new people in charge wanted to get rid of the old ways of doing things. It was a time of huge change in France. The monarchy was abolished and replaced by a system of government that tried to make life fairer for everyone.

kilo-	hecto-	deca-	g m ℓ		deci-	centi-	milli-
1000	100	10			0.1	0.01	0.001

The metric system

The French defined a universal way of measuring and counting. They asked scientists to develop a decimal system of measurements, which means a system based on the number 10. This "metric" system was not popular straightaway, but its ease of use saw it gradually spread around the world. The invention of the meter and the kilogram were of particular importance. Today, most countries use the metric system of weights and measures, which presents multiples of 10, as you can see in 1,000 for kilogram, for example.

The imperial system

Some older systems of weights and measures are still in use today, alongside or instead of the metric system. The imperial system was defined in the British Weights and Measures Act of 1824, and set as a standard throughout the British Empire. In Great Britain and the United States, scientists measure distances in centimeters, meters, and kilometers, but road signs still use the old, imperial system of feet and miles.

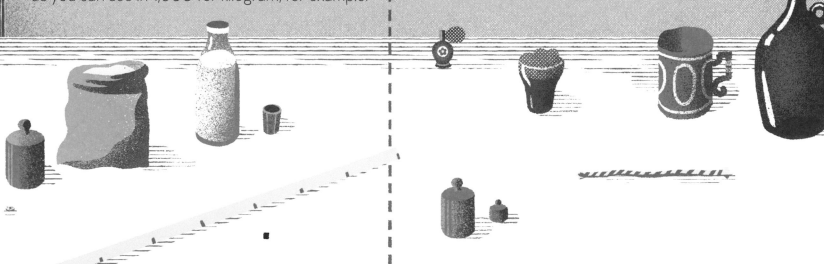

From the North Pole to the equator:
the invention of the meter

Before the French Revolution there were many different systems of
measuring distances that people had devised in the centuries before.
The new universal unit of length, the meter, replaced these in 1793.
It was very tricky to get it right at first, but the meter has become
the world's standard unit for measuring length.

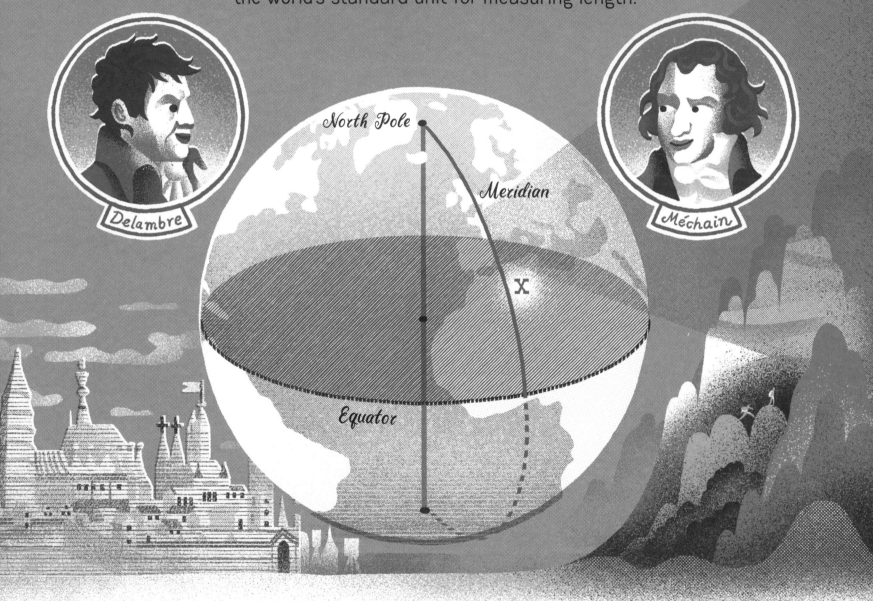

Measuring the size of the Earth

The French Academy of Sciences decided that the meter should be based on the size of the Earth. In order
to do so, two scientists, Pierre-François-André Méchain and Jean-Baptiste Delambre, set out to measure
the distance between the equator (an imaginary circle around the Earth, right in the middle between the
North and South poles) and the North Pole along a straight line (called the meridian) running through Paris.

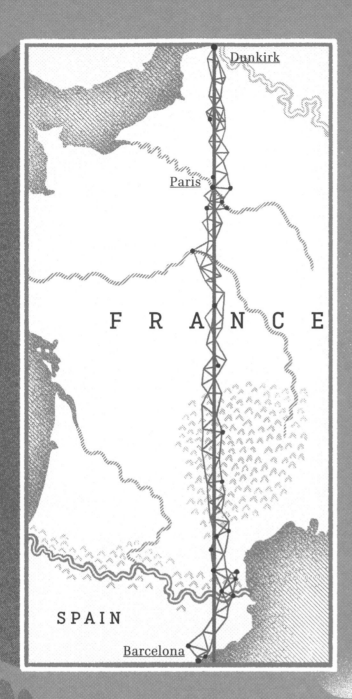

From Dunkirk to Barcelona

It was too difficult to travel to the North Pole to measure the distance between the poles, but Méchain and Delambre figured out a trick: They chose a small section of the meridian, running from Dunkirk in the north of France to Barcelona in Spain. By measuring the distance between the two cities and taking into account the curvature of the Earth, they could work out the total length.

$$\frac{X}{10\ 000\ 000} = \textit{mètre}$$

A new standard

It took the two scientists more than six years to complete their task. The final result, measured in an older unit called a *toise*, was divided by 10,000,000 to create the new measure: the *mètre*. The French made a 1 meter bar out of platinum, a precious metal, and placed it in the National Archives in Paris. Copies of it were later sent to other countries, but it took another 150 years before most of the world accepted the meter as the standard.

Kilometers and millimeters

Using the meter as the starting point, we can today measure any length, from the distance you travel on your way to school to the microscopic size of bacteria cells. Bigger distances are often measured in kilometers (1 km = 1,000 meters), while smaller things are measured in millimeters (1 mm = 1,000th of a meter).

A new standard for mass: the kilogram

Having set a new standard measure for distances, French scientists went on to do the same for measuring mass. The new unit, called the kilogram, was based on the weight of a 10 cm by 10 cm cube filled with one liter of water. Because water's density depends on the temperature, they choose the freezing point, when water turns to ice.

Most people in Europe used to calculate the mass of goods in pounds, a measure derived from the ancient Roman unit the *libra* (the Latin for "scales"). The problem was that many countries and regions developed their own versions of the pound, which made trading across borders very complicated. One pound of silver in England was very different from a pound of gold in Germany, for example.

1000 cm³

10 cm
10 cm
10 cm

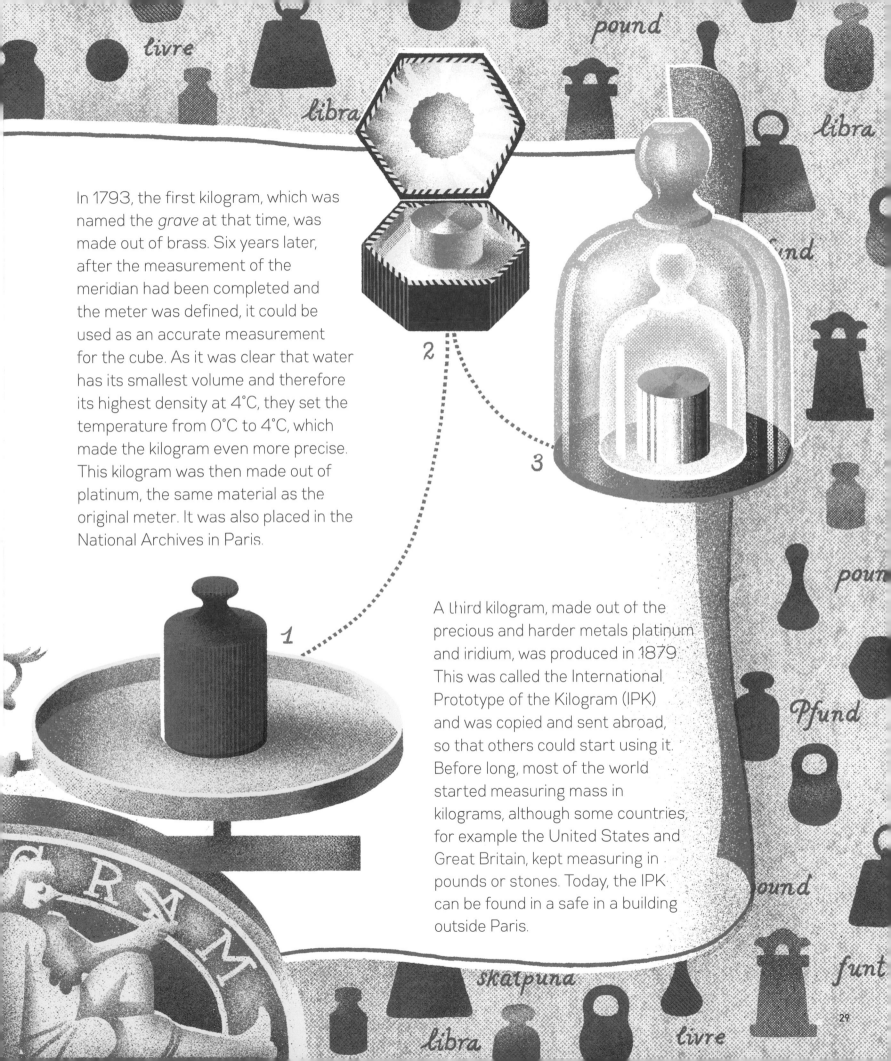

In 1793, the first kilogram, which was named the *grave* at that time, was made out of brass. Six years later, after the measurement of the meridian had been completed and the meter was defined, it could be used as an accurate measurement for the cube. As it was clear that water has its smallest volume and therefore its highest density at 4°C, they set the temperature from 0°C to 4°C, which made the kilogram even more precise. This kilogram was then made out of platinum, the same material as the original meter. It was also placed in the National Archives in Paris.

A third kilogram, made out of the precious and harder metals platinum and iridium, was produced in 1879. This was called the International Prototype of the Kilogram (IPK) and was copied and sent abroad, so that others could start using it. Before long, most of the world started measuring mass in kilograms, although some countries, for example the United States and Great Britain, kept measuring in pounds or stones. Today, the IPK can be found in a safe in a building outside Paris.

Grains, seashells, coins:
the invention of money

If you get pocket money, you know how it works: you can use it to buy things or save it to get something bigger in the future. But why was money invented and how did people pay for things before there were coins and paper money?

Before money

In the early days of humanity, people exchanged goods and services directly with each other. This was called bartering. A Stone Age man might have offered his mammoth-fur coat to someone in exchange for an axe, for example. But bartering wasn't always possible. Maybe the man with the axe already had a very nice fur coat and needed a new blanket instead?

Things as money

Trading became a little smoother once people agreed to accept everyday things that everybody needed—animals or even grain—as payment. In some places, people used seashells as money. But this was still impractical, because the value of such things changed from place to place, person to person.

Coins and notes

The answer was to make coins from gold or silver that people could exchange for goods and services. The ancient Lydians were one of the first peoples to mint coins, in about 700 BC. A few hundred years later, the Chinese started making money as paper notes. Large sums could be carried more easily that way.

Today's money

The coins and paper money you get for your pocket money today have value because everybody accepts them, just as most people will accept payment by card—the transfer of money in digital form, directly from your bank account to theirs.

31

How hot is hot? How scientists came up with a cool way to measure temperature

If you jump into a swimming pool on a hot summer's day, the water will feel cold. But on a cold day, the same water will feel quite warm! The human body is very good at picking up on quick changes in temperature through nerves in the skin, but when the temperature stays the same, everybody feels differently. Some children might shiver going to school without a jacket in springtime, while their friends would feel too hot wearing one; what's warm to one person might be cold to another. Therefore, to find the true temperature, people had to develop a way of measuring it.

The earliest instruments used for measuring temperature–called thermometers–were invented by the ancient Romans and looked at the way water reacted to heat. But it wasn't until 1714 that a more reliable way was invented by the German physicist Daniel Gabriel Fahrenheit.

Fahrenheit replaced water with quicksilver, a liquid metal that expands when it gets warm. His temperature scale refers to a mix of ice, water, and salt for 0 Fahrenheit, the melting point of water at 32 Fahrenheit, and the temperature of the human body at 96 Fahrenheit.

The rule of thumb to convert from Fahrenheit to Celsius: Take the number in Fahrenheit, subtract 30, divide the result by 2, and you will get Celsius.

Later, the Fahrenheit scale was changed to set the freezing point of water at 32 Fahrenheit and the boiling point of water at 212 Fahrenheit–a difference of 180 degrees. In the United States and a handful of other countries, the Fahrenheit (degree Fahrenheit or °F) is still used to measure temperature.

°F | °C

Most nations, however, have adopted a different system: Celsius (degree Celsius or °C), named after the Swedish scientist Anders Celsius. In 1742, Celsius invented a scale that started with 100 degrees for the freezing point of water and went down to 0 degree for the boiling point of water. These two points were flipped later on to how we use them today. Because Celsius is much easier to use than Fahrenheit, it became the more popular system.

Even though Fahrenheit was German, Germans use Celsius to measure temperature, like almost everybody else.

Sun and summer, night and winter:
the origin of time and calendars

Having invented numbers to keep track of objects, people also had to come up with ways of keeping track of time. They did so by observing the regular changes that occur in the natural world: the rising and setting of the Sun every day; blooming flowers in spring, red and yellow leaves on the trees in fall; animals hibernating during the cold of winter.

People have always been interested in the changing seasons because they needed to know the right times for planting and harvesting crops. But those natural signs were not foolproof. A warmer winter might trick a farmer into planting crops too early. If the new seedlings were then killed by frost, it could lead to famine. As civilizations grew, people needed a much more reliable way to track what time of year it was.

The calendar we use today developed slowly over the past 5,000 years. To understand its roots, we have to look at the different calendars developed by earlier civilizations.

APRIL

			1	2	3	4
5	6	7	8	9	10	11
12	13	14	15	16	17	18
19	20	21	22	23	24	25
26	27	28	29	30		

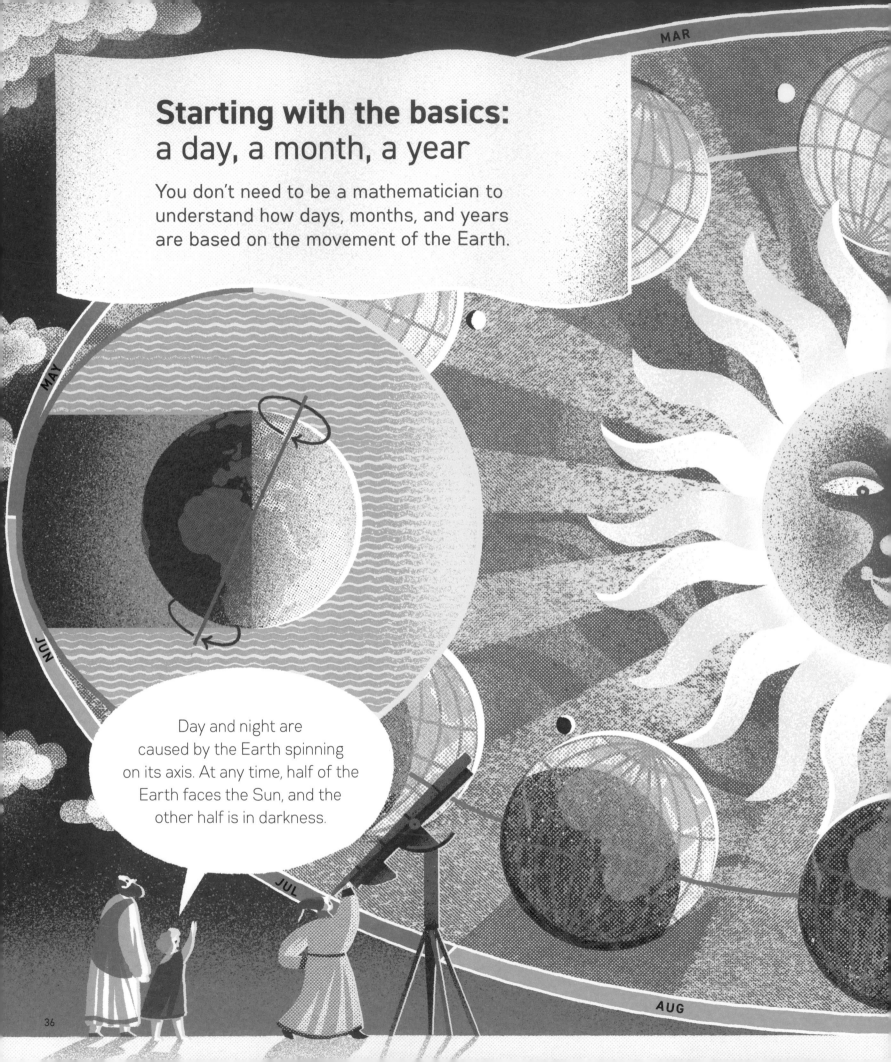

Starting with the basics:
a day, a month, a year

You don't need to be a mathematician to understand how days, months, and years are based on the movement of the Earth.

Day and night are caused by the Earth spinning on its axis. At any time, half of the Earth faces the Sun, and the other half is in darkness.

A month is how long it takes the Moon to circle the Earth.

A year is how long it takes the Earth to move around the Sun.

Taken together, the Earth, Sun, and Moon are the basis for the calendar.

37

Stones, stars, and the Moon: how ancient peoples came up with different calendars

A calendar is a system for naming days and grouping them together into longer periods of time. Early calendars differed from place to place, depending on the reasons why people wanted to track time.

Ancient monuments, such as Stonehenge in England, may have been built to observe the changing seasons by tracking the position of the Sun in the sky. The rising or setting Sun lines up with different stones at certain times of the year.

In ancient Egypt, star patterns were used to make the first calendars. Life was centered on the River Nile: its regular flooding made the dry desert soil fertile enough to grow crops. The ancient Egyptians noticed that a star called Sirius appeared in the same place in the sky just before each flood, notifying them to get ready. They worked out that this happened every 365 days.

The Babylonians noticed that the sliver of the Moon got bigger and smaller every 30 days or so. They based their year on 12 complete cycles of the Moon. Each cycle starts with a crescent Moon at sunset. These cycles are the basis for what we now call a month.

The modern calendar:
a 500-year-old invention

In ancient Greece, they had calendars based on both the Sun and the Moon. Twelve Moon cycles, or "months" of 30 days each, added up to 360 days. In comparison, a solar year, which is based on the position of the Sun in the sky, was about 365 days long. To bridge the gap of those five days, the clever ancient Greeks added an extra month: In a span of 19 years, the first 12 years had 12 months, and the last 7 years had 13 months.

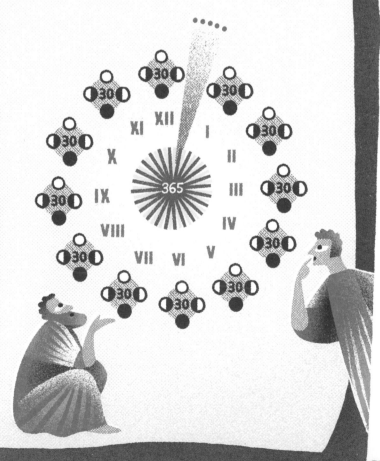

In ancient Rome, Julius Caesar introduced a calendar that made the year 365 days long, with an extra day every four years to keep the calendar in sync with the Sun—this year is called a leap year. That calendar had 12 months, based on complete cycles of the Moon. The Roman Empire was so powerful that this calendar, called the Julian calendar, spread throughout Europe. Today, this extra day is February 29.

By the 1500s, the Julian calendar was lagging 10 days behind the Sun because the actual length of a solar year is 365 days, 5 hours, and approximately 49 minutes. To make up for that flaw, Pope Gregory XIII set some mathematicians and astronomers the task of solving this surplus of 5 hours and 49 minutes. The solution meant that, every few hundred years, a leap year would have to be skipped, meaning that instead of every four years, there would be an eight-year gap. They decided to skip the leap years on the first year of each century, but only if that number was not divisible by 400. So, this means we had a leap year in 2000 (2000 ÷ 400 = 5), but won't in 2100 (2100 ÷ 400 = 5.25). Most of the world, including us, still uses this Gregorian calendar today.

1582 OCTOBRIS 1582

1	2	3	4	15	16
17	18	1.		21	22	23
24	25		28	29	30
31					

1500 1600 1700 1800 1900 2000 2100 2200 2300

Other calendars are still being used alongside the Gregorian one that are even more closely linked to the movements and appearance of the Moon. Millions of people in China use the traditional Chinese calendar to determine dates for holidays, weddings, and even funerals. The Chinese New Year doesn't start on January 1 like the Gregorian New Year does, but falls on a different day in winter (between January 21 and February 21) each year. The Jewish calendar is also used to determine dates for religious rituals. In this, New Year refers to the harvest season in September or October. It marks the end of the agricultural year and the start of a new one.

Time's up! One world, one clock

When do you have to get up in the morning in order to get to school on time? When are you going over to your best friend's house? How long do you have left to read in bed until it's "lights out"? To know the time, all you have to do is take a quick look at the clock. But the numbers—the hours, minutes, and seconds—we use today have come a very long way. This is how they came about.

Position of the Sun

In Europe, it was common for a village or town to have just one clock, often displayed on a tall clock tower. The time on these clocks was set according to the Sun: midday was whenever it was highest in the sky and not at 12 p.m. as it is today. This meant that even towns and cities in the same country kept different times. They could be a few minutes or even a few hours apart.

This made life difficult. Should a train or boat journey be timed from the place it started from or the place it arrived? If you arranged to meet someone at 6 p.m., was that your time or their time? At first, people dealt with this by changing their timepieces as they traveled. Coaching companies even printed information sheets on how and when to change your watch.

Setting the clock

However, British railway companies wanted a better solution —a single standard time that was the same across the country. In 1847, Greenwich Mean Time (GMT)—the time at Greenwich, London—was chosen as the standard time for rail schedules across Great Britain. It became known as Railway Time.

By the late 1800s, people had realized it would be useful to have a standard time to refer to wherever you were in the world. The United States and most of the world's sea charts were already using GMT as the basis for working out the time. So, in 1884, Greenwich Mean Time was chosen as the international standard.

AMBER GATE, NOTTINGHAM AND BOSTON, AND ___ JUNCTION RAILWAY.— Notice is Hereby Given, that the RAILWAY from N___ ___HAM to GRANTHAM will be OPENED for PUBLIC PASSENGER TRAFFIC on MONDA___

TIME-TABLE FOR JULY,

GREENWICH TIME IS KEPT AT ALL THE STAT.

It's night—and day.
Why we have time zones

When you're going to bed, somewhere else in the world another child will be getting up or having their lunch. Because the Earth constantly spins in space, the Sun rises and sets at different times in different places. Somewhere in the world, it's morning, lunchtime, or evening. Most countries use a single hourly time zone to make life simpler. But a few countries, such as the United States, are so large that different regions or states have their own, separate time zones.

-11 — -10 — -9 — -8 — -7 — -6 — -5 — -4 — -3 — -2 — -1

Each line on the globe on the left indicates a 15-degree spin of the Earth on its axis, which takes 1 hour. Everyone inside the same zone sets their clock to the same time.

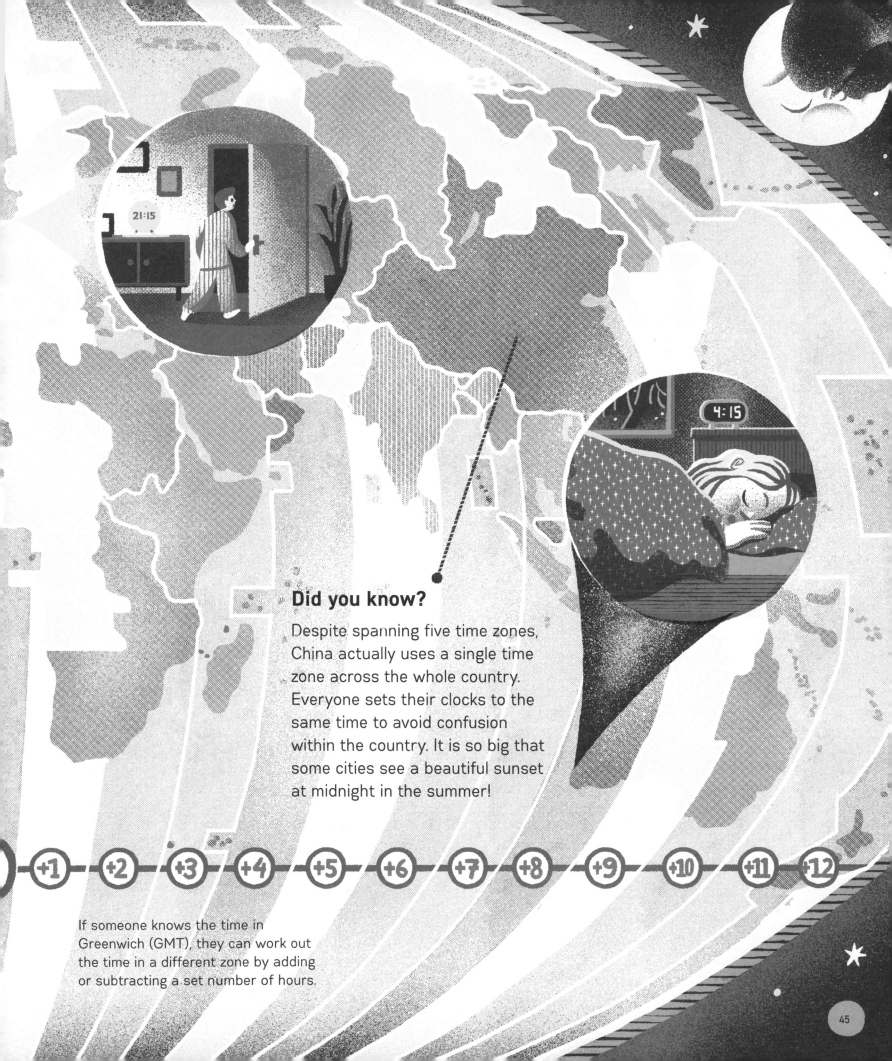

Did you know?

Despite spanning five time zones, China actually uses a single time zone across the whole country. Everyone sets their clocks to the same time to avoid confusion within the country. It is so big that some cities see a beautiful sunset at midnight in the summer!

+1 +2 +3 +4 +5 +6 +7 +8 +9 +10 +11 +12

If someone knows the time in Greenwich (GMT), they can work out the time in a different zone by adding or subtracting a set number of hours.

24 hours, 60 minutes, 60 seconds:
how humans came up with a system to measure time

A day is the time it takes our planet to spin once on its axis–you can't argue with this huge rock spinning through space! But why did humans decide there should be 24 hours in a day, with 60 minutes in an hour, and 60 seconds in a minute? They needed to make a connection between the Earth and its spinning on its axis. So they started to measure the Earth itself!

Dividing the day into 24 parts

About 3,500 years ago, the ancient Egyptians began using the length and direction of shadows to work out how much of the day was still left. They used these shadow measurements to divide their days into 12 parts, and the position of the stars to divide the night into 12, creating the 24-hour day. Those were a bit like our hours today, but with one big difference: they were longer in summer (when the Sun was in the sky for longer) and shorter in winter.

Measuring the Earth

An interim stage of measuring time happened approximately 2,260 years ago, when the ancient Greek astronomer Eratosthenes estimated the Earth's circumference (the distance around the whole planet). Using the Babylonian counting system that was popular with scientists at the time, he divided this giant circle into 60 parts, creating the first measure of latitude. The counting system of 60 is more versatile than using base 10, and more flexible, since it's easy to find fractions of 60, which divides neatly by 2, 3, 4, 5, and 6. This comes in handy when you want to divide a circle into 360 degrees, a year into 360 days, an hour into 60 minutes, a minute into 60 seconds–or the Earth itself, as Eratosthenes did.

From approximate to accurate

As the "hours" used by the ancient Egyptians were longer in the summer and shorter in the winter, in about 140 BC the ancient Greek astronomer Hipparchus began looking for a more accurate way to record the movements of the Sun, Moon, and stars in the sky. He proposed to split up the 24 hours of a day into equal length. For that Hipparchus divided it vertically from pole to pole with 360 imaginary lines (while Eratosthenes divided the Earth's surface horizontally) and created the Earth's longitude.

Minutes and seconds

The ancient Greek astronomer Ptolemy went a step further, splitting each of the 360 degrees of latitude and longitude into 60 equal parts, each of which was subdivided into 60 smaller parts—probably to fix positions of place more precisely. This convention of degrees, minutes, and seconds is still used today to plot locations on the Earth as well as the positions of stars. Many centuries later, the "first" 60 segments ended up being our minutes, and the "second" smaller segments became the seconds as we use them today for everyday timekeeping.

How to count in 60s

The Babylonians liked counting based on the number 60, which was invented by the Sumerians 6,000 years ago. To count like a Sumerian, use your right thumb to count each phalanx on your left hand. Fold your thumb down, then do the same with your index finger, and repeat using each of the five fingers on your right hand.

$5 \times 12 = 60$

Hold on a second!
A lot of things can happen in the blink of an eye

You can blink in a second. Let's see what else can happen in that moment ...

The Earth travels 30km (18 mi) while orbiting the Sun.

The fastest person in the world can run 10.4 m.

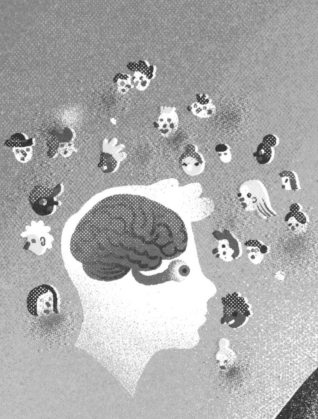

Your brain can process nearly 77 different images seen by your eyes—for example, when you scan a crowd to look for someone you know.

55

50

45

6

Light from the Sun travels about 300,000 km (186,000 mi) through space—that's almost all the way from the Earth to the Moon!

The International Space Station travels 8 km (5 mi) in its orbit around the Earth.

Hummingbirds have been known to flap their wings more than 70 times per second, while their hearts can beat up to 21 times.

The world's fastest computer performs 143 quadrillion calculations.

Patterns and numbers:
Understanding nature

There is a fascinating connection between nature and numbers.
Certain numbers and sequences appear everywhere.

The Fibonacci sequence

Some things in nature repeat in a certain sequence. The Italian
mathematician Fibonacci, one of the greatest mathematicians to have
lived, came across the Hindu-Arabic numerals while visiting Algeria.

Using the numbers from 0 to 9 allowed
Fibonacci to explore math in a whole new way.
He is most famous for this sequence of numbers
that bears his name: 0, 1, 1, 2, 3, 5, 8, 13, 21, 34 …

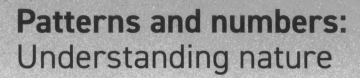

0 – 1 – 1 – 2 – 3 – 5 – 8 – 13 – 21 – 34 – S

Each new number in the sequence is
found by adding the two numbers before
it—so 0+1=1, 1+1=2, 1+2=3, 2+3=5,
and so on. Fibonacci developed the
sequence while trying to work out how
many rabbits could be born in a year if a
rabbit breeder started with a single pair
of rabbits. Although rabbit breeding
doesn't actually follow Fibonacci's rule,
the number pattern he discovered does
pop up everywhere in nature.

$$\frac{c}{d} = \pi$$

3.1415926535 89

∞

Infinity (∞) is not a number. It's used to represent the idea of something that never ends or has no limits. This is useful in math, for example, for describing how you could go on counting forever or cutting something in half forever! It's also used in physics, to describe the idea that both time and space go on forever.

π (pi)

If you take any circle and divide its circumference (the distance around the outside) by its diameter (the distance across the circle), the answer will always be the same: 3.1415926535 ... –pi (π) for short. The digits after the decimal place seem to go on forever. Powerful computer programs have worked out more than 31 trillion digits, but have found no repeating pattern. Circles are all around us in nature, so π helps to describe how the world works.

φ (phi) and the golden ratio

The golden ratio is a mathematical proportion that appears throughout nature, such as in the spirals of snail shells and the pattern of seeds in a sunflower, and has inspired many famous works of art and design, including the Great Pyramid of Giza. This mathematical proportion is defined by a special number: phi (φ), or 1.618034.

You can see this in the rectangle on the right. Draw a line through that rectangle to create a square inside it (a). The space left over (b) beside that square will also be rectangle in the exact same ratio as the original rectangle you started with. You achieve the perfect harmony between both lines when a ÷ b = phi.

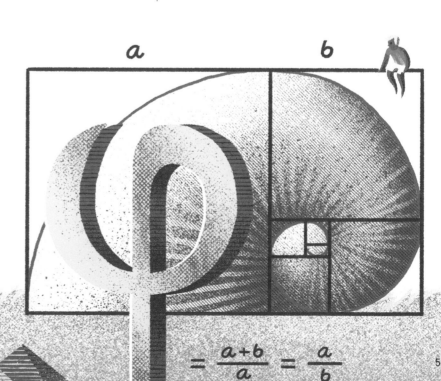

$$= \frac{a+b}{a} = \frac{a}{b}$$

0s and 1s: why do computers only use two numbers?

While our brains can cope with nine digits and zero (the decimal system), computers use a much simpler number system. Amazingly, computer-coding roots go back hundreds of years before computers were invented. In 1679, the German mathematician Gottfried Wilhelm Leibniz invented a binary number system, a way to write down numbers using just two digits: 0 and 1.

How to write the numbers
0 to 10 in binary:

The binary system uses columns, starting with the number 1, and doubling each time, from right to left. That's what the red numbers are at the top of this board.

8	4	2	1	
0	0	0	0	0
0	0	0	1	1
0	0	1	0	2
0	0	1	1	3
0	1	0	0	4
0	1	0	1	5
0	1	1	0	6
0	1	1	1	7
1	0	0	0	8
1	0	0	1	9
1	0	1	0	10

To write the selected number (in blue) in binary code, you activate the red numbers at the top using 1s and 0s (in green), 1 being on, 0 being off.

So, to write the number 5, we need to activate a 4 and a 1 (because 4+1=5). You can see those columns are activated, while the rest show a 0. To show larger numbers, more columns need to be added, and the codes will become longer and longer.

Here is the alphabet translated into binary code. Can you write your name in binary?

A	1000001	N	1001110
B	1000010	O	1001111
C	1000011	P	1010000
D	1000100	Q	1010001
E	1000101	R	1010010
F	1000110	S	1010011
G	1000111	T	1010100
H	1001000	U	1010101
I	1001001	V	1010110
J	1001010	W	1010111
K	1001011	X	1011000
L	1001100	Y	1011001
M	1001101	Z	1011010

When people began developing computers more than 200 years later, the binary system was perfectly suited to help people "talk" to computers. The two digits—0 and 1—could match the flow of electricity being off (0) or on (1).

No matter what type of computer code, or programming language, is used to write an app or a computer game, it is always translated into simple binary code. This is the language of computers.

Ada Lovelace

1815 - 1852

A talented mathematician, Ada Lovelace was fascinated by the "calculating machines" that were invented in the 1800s and studied the mathematics behind them. She realized that, one day, "computers" would be able to do much more than work out the results of long sums. She correctly predicted that they would be able to handle any data that could be coded using numbers, including music and pictures. One hundred years later, her predictions came true. She is now remembered as one of the first computer programmers.

Code crackers! Turning messages into numbers and back again

A code is a sequence of numbers or signals that carry a specific message. Codes are often secret and can only be read if you know exactly how they work.

Can you break this code?*

YM TAC SI YRGNUH

Morse code

Letters and numbers are translated into dots and dashes.

A	U
B	V
C	W
D	X
E	Y
F	Z
G	
H	
I	
J	
K	1
L	2
M	3
N	4
O	5
P	6
Q	7
R	8
S	9
T	0

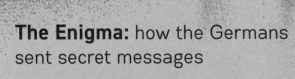

Some of the most famous codebreakers in history were mathematicians! Cracking codes and deciphering secret messages involve a lot of math. At the beginning of the Second World War, many of Great Britain's top mathematicians, including Alan Turing and Joan Clarke, were asked to help crack coded messages sent between the Germans. They all worked together at a secret location called Bletchley Park, using some incredible mathematical machines!

The Enigma: how the Germans sent secret messages

At first, Turing and Clarke worked on secret messages being sent by the German army that were written with the help of an Enigma machine. The machine had billions of different settings that were changed every day. Enigma codes were thought to be unbreakable and were therefore used to send very important information, for example, the exact time and location of an attack by bomber planes.

*Read each word backward.

The Bombe: reading and decoding messages

Turing was good enough at math to spot patterns in the coded messages and work out what those rules were. He helped to design a mechanical machine called Bombe, which could help others to crack Enigma codes more quickly. Even with the help of the machine it was hard and slow work, however. It took Clarke and her colleagues three months using Bombe to read six days of messages sent by enemy forces.

The Colossus: cracking the code

By 1944, the mathematicians at Bletchley Park had constructed an electronic machine to crack the most important German messages, which were being sent using binary code. Colossus could carry out millions of calculations in a much shorter space of time than Bombe. It was the world's first large-scale electronic computer. Because it helped the British and their allies work out the Germans' plans in advance, it helped to end the war more quickly.

Numbers are endless.
And so are the possibilities

If you think math is tricky, imagine being a Sumerian and counting in base 60! If you find it hard to get to school on time, imagine being a Roman and only having a sundial to refer to!

Numbers begin with counting, but it goes much further than that. Once we understand the relationship, we can start to use numbers to make sense of our world.

Numbers and time are human inventions that help to organize the lives of the Earth's 7.7 billion people and keep the human world running "like clockwork." But they do much more than that. Uncovering the mathematical patterns hidden in nature helps us to explain the history of our planet, and all of its living things.

By building on our mathematical understanding over hundreds of years, we have been able to use numbers to build skyscrapers, design computers, send humans to the Moon—and robots far beyond.

But we don't know everything yet. There are still "impossible" problems to solve and secrets of the universe to be unlocked.

What will you discover?

Glossary

Abacus: A simple frame with rows of wires that beads can slide along. It can be used to count, add, multiply, and subtract.

Ancient Greece: a civilization that started about 700 BC and developed until the Romans conquered Greece in the year 146 BC. It is considered the origin of Western culture.

Ancient Rome: a powerful empire that ruled most of Europe for nearly 1,000 years.

Artificial light: light produced by electric lamps.

Astronomy: the scientific study of all objects outside the Earth's atmosphere. These include the Sun, Moon, planets, stars, galaxies, and all other matter in the universe.

Axis: a real or imaginary line through the center of an object, around which the object turns.

Babylon: the capital city of the ancient kingdom of Babylonia, in Mesopotamia.

Babylonian: a native person, or inhabitant, of ancient Babylonia.

Binary system: a numeral system that writes numbers using only 0 and 1.

Calculations: the method or result of adding, subtracting, multiplying, or dividing.

Carob tree: an evergreen tree with red flowers and edible pods.

Coding: creating a system of instructions that tells a computer what to do.

Cuneiform: A written language used by the Sumerians and the Babylonians. It was made up of marks or letters shaped like wedges.

Currency: The system used to exchange things. Each country or area has its own.

Cycle: A period of time with a beginning and an end, in which something happens. Once it finishes, it starts again.

Data: a collection of information.

Decimal system or **Hindu-Arabic numeral system:** A number system that has 10 digits to show all the numbers. It uses 0, 1, 2, 3, 4, 5, 6, 7, 8, and 9.

Digits: symbols used to make numerals.

Fractions: the parts of a group, number, or whole.

French Revolution: a period in France when the people overthrew the monarchy and took control of the government.

Geometry: an area of mathematics that studies the size, shape, and positions of things with points, lines, and angles.

Goods: something that is useful for people and has a value, and therefore can be bought and sold.

Great Pyramid of Giza: a huge pyramid built by the ancient Egyptians near Cairo, Egypt.

Gregorian calendar: The calendar that is used most throughout the world. It was introduced in 1582 by Pope Gregory XIII.

Imperial system: an old system of measurement units developed in Great Britain.

Lydians: the native people, or inhabitants, of the ancient kingdom of Lydia, in Anatolia.

Measurements: the value of something, defined by its size, shape, length, etc., and discovered through the act of measuring.

Mesopotamia: an ancient region of land that is now part of Iraq.

Metric system: a system of measurement based on units of 10.

Monarchy: a form of government in which one person, the king or queen, has the maximum power.

North Pole: the most northern point of the Earth's axis.

Number system: a set of numbers or symbols that are used to represent numbers.

Numeral: a symbol or name that represents a number.

Orbit: the path that an object takes in space as it goes around a planet, a moon, or a star.

Philosophy: the study of the basic ideas of human life.

Programmers: people who write computer programs.

Quantities: the different amounts of things.

Solar year: a year made up of 365 days, based on the position of the Sun in the sky.

Service: an activity that one person does, and can be of useful, helpful, or create value for someone else.

Sumerian: a native person, or inhabitant, of Sumer.

Sumer: the earliest known civilization in southern Mesopotamia, now southern Iraq.

Time zone: an area on the Earth that has a specific time that all the local citizens can set their clocks to.

Trade: the buying and selling of goods.

Volume: the amount of space something occupies, taking into account its height, length, and width.

In Great Numbers
How Numbers Shape the World we Live in

Illustrated by Daniela Olejníková
Written by Isabel Thomas, Robert Klanten, Maria-Elisabeth Niebius,
and Raphael Honigstein

This book was conceived, edited, and designed by Little Gestalten

Edited by Robert Klanten and Maria-Elisabeth Niebius

Design and layout by Emily Sear

Fact-checking by Kathrin Lilienthal

Typefaces: Gabriel Sans; DIN 2014 by Vasily Biryukov

Printed by die Keure, Bruges
Made in Europe

Published by Little Gestalten, Berlin 2020
ISBN 978-3-89955-820-3

For more information, and to order books, please visit www.little.gestalten.com.

Bibliographic information published by the Deutsche Nationalbibliothek.
The Deutsche Nationalbibliothek lists this publication in the Deutsche
Nationalbibliografie; detailed bibliographic data are available online at www.dnb.de.

This book was printed on paper certified according to the standards of the FSC®.